Destined

for

HEALING

DESTINED FOR HEALING
Marty Delmon

Published by:

RPJ & COMPANY, INC.
Post Office Box 160243 | Altamonte Springs, Florida 32716-0243 | 407.551.0734
Web site: www.rpjandco.com

First printing, June 2009
Updated, February 2011

ISBN-13: 978-0-9828277-1-0
ISBN-10: 0-9828277-1-7

Cover and Interior Layout & Design:
RPJ & Company, Inc.
www.rpjandco.com

Cover Image of Jumping on the beach © IKO - Fotolia.com

Scripture taken from the New King James Version, unless otherwise noted. Copyright © 1982 by Thomas Nelson, Inc. Used by permission. All rights reserved.

Printed in the United States of America.

Destined

for

HEALING

Marty Delmon

Published by:

RPJ & COMPANY, INC.
www.rpjandco.com

Table of Contents

Healing Belongs to Us. 7

How to Obtain Healing 17

Current Mentality About Healing 33

Why Some People Aren't Healed and/or
Why Some People Lose their Healing 55

What About Death: When Do We Stop
Believing for Someone Else's Healing? 69

The Healings of Jesus. 81

Will He find Faith? 87

A Message from the Author 91

More Books 94

Chapter 1

Healing Belongs to Us

As a mother of two young children and needing to be economical as well as to feed my kids nourishing protein, I bought a chunk of meat on sale. Wanting to cut it into bite size pieces and make a stew, I took a serrated knife, put the meat on a chopping board and began the task. It amazed me how tough one slab of meat could be.

It took all of my muscular strength to cut through the sinews and gristle. I gripped that meat in one hand, my fingers acting like claws holding it in place while I sawed with the other hand, my body swinging back and forth with the effort. I heard, rather than felt, the knife working itself on a bone, yet my fingers didn't feel any bones in the meat.

Suddenly I realized it was MY bone! I was gripping the meat so hard that my fingers had become a part of it and the knife sliced back and forth on my own bone. Horrified, I dropped the meat, the knife skittered on the floor as I held my hand in front of my face watching the blood spurt from my left forefinger across the kitchen splatting on the cabinets and the countertops.

Grabbing the finger, I put pressure on the cut to stop the blood from literally shooting out in arced streams. I started to panic when I heard a voice inside of me say, "You don't have to put up with this."

The words "put up with this," stunned me. My logical mind instantly responded with, "Why not? I did it to myself." Fortunately, I responded to the voice instead of to my logic. I brought both hands, one still grasping the finger, in front of my face and yelled at it. "I don't have to put up with this! Stop! You stop! Right this minute!"

Wondering what else to say I heard the voice again, "Tell it to be healed."

Again I shouted, "Be healed! In the name of Jesus! Be healed! You stop bleeding! You grow back together right now!" I continued speaking like this to my finger, actually shouting, frantic to maintain this spiritual pitch, wanting to obtain a healing as much as to respond to the prompting from my heart.

The next cue I received was to release the finger, which I did. The spurting had stopped and as I watched, in silence now, the skin came back together before my eyes and did not leave even so much as a scar, a wrinkle or a line to ever prove something had happened. The only evidence was the blood coagulating all over my kitchen.

This was my first experience with Divine Healing. Since then I've had many healings; some have left a small mark, kind of like a reminder of how blessed I am that Healing belongs to me, but most leave no trace, only complete restoration.

When Jesus suffered so excruciatingly for us during His beatings, the carrying of the cross, the crucifixion and His death, burial and resurrection, He purchased SALVATION for us. This word, salvation, basically means to be saved from anything that is negative or nasty. Anything that steals life, destroys or kills, that is what Jesus paid for with His body and His blood.

We can make a sentence starting with 'I've been saved from…' and then fill in the space with whatever steals, kills and destroys. Sickness and disease are things that steal, kill and destroy. And yes, we have been saved from sickness and disease. This book is to demonstrate that truth and to explain how to use the healing that belongs to us.

"Surely He has borne our griefs and carried our sorrows yet we esteemed Him stricken, smitten by God and afflicted, but He was wounded for our transgressions, He was bruised for our iniquities,

the chastisement for our peace was upon Him, and
by His stripes we are healed" (Isaiah 53:4-5).

This Scripture verse is a prophetic word. Isaiah spoke
for God. He foretold what Jesus would do for us when
He suffered through all the stages of the crucifixion and
resurrection. The Amplified Bible tells us that the word
"griefs" means "sicknesses, weaknesses, and distresses."
These words refer to physical life, not spiritual life.

The word "sorrows" in this Scripture means "pains."
In His flesh, when He was beaten, Jesus took upon His
body the sicknesses, weaknesses, distresses and pains of
our bodies while we are living on this earth. We won't
need these healings after we die. Heaven is a perfect place.
There won't be any of these things in heaven so Jesus
couldn't have carried something for us that we will never
experience there.

Some claim that although Jesus healed people while
on the earth, the only healing that remains for us today is
spiritual healing. But consider when He did this. The time
when He carried our sicknesses, weaknesses, distresses and
pains was on His body on the cross when there was no time
left for Him to actually do the healing. He did not come
down from the cross and lay hands on anyone. In fact, right
after He took these works of the devil on His body, He died.
Therefore, who is the "we" that Isaiah 53:5 talked about?
Who is the "we" who was healed by His stripes? Isn't it all
those who came after the cross?

He was "stricken, smitten by God and afflicted," "wounded," "bruised" and "chastised." These things were done to His body so our bodies wouldn't have to suffer. Have you ever taken the punishment for someone else? In a certain family I know, it was customary, when the child was naughty, for the youngster to cut a supple branch from a bush in the yard for his spanking.

One time the father asked his son to cut a switch because he had been naughty. But when the child returned to the house, already in tears for the whipping he would get with that lash, the father got down on his hands and knees. He said, "I want you to spank me with that switch, son."

The boy asked, "Why? I'm the one who deserves to be punished."

The father softly replied, "I know. And someone has to be punished for what you've done. I'm going to take your punishment."

"But why?" the boy cried.

"Jesus took our punishments. He took our sickness and disease away and He paid for our sins. So I'm going to pay for yours."

The boy cried and cried, but he could not bring himself to whip his father. "Please, Daddy, I'll never, ever do it again."

Right after being born again, there was abhorrence in my soul for my former sins. I didn't even know enough to ask to be forgiven; however, I discovered that I was and that I didn't want to sin again. Like that little boy, I can't imagine asking Jesus to suffer and die for me. But He did.

I think it's time we accepted His sacrifice. When we get born again, we never question our salvation after that initial experience. We give our hearts to Jesus; His Holy Spirit comes to live inside of us and we know it is a done deal. Never again do we have to go through the New Birth. We've been born into the Kingdom of God as His children and we know we belong to Him.

Healing came with that gift of salvation. 'Well, if that's so,' you might ask, 'then how come we don't question our salvation; we always have it, but we have to obtain healing over and over again?' I'm presenting to you, in this book, the fact that you don't have to obtain healing over and over again if you receive it in the first place as easily as you received your eternal life with God. The truth is: we hold healing in a state of unbelief.

The Bible says we didn't comprehend His sacrifice. We don't see that He did it for our bodies. Like verse 4 of Isaiah 53 says, we stop short in our reasoning and do not realize all He accomplished for us through His suffering. His blood bought us and paid for our sins, but His body bought and paid for our sicknesses and diseases.

The last phrase says it: "by His stripes I am healed." Peter repeats that phrase, quoting Isaiah in I Peter 2:24,

Who Himself bore my sins in His own body on the tree that I having died to sins might live for righteousness by whose stripes I am healed.

Matthew talks about Jesus healing people and he also quotes Isaiah in 8:17,

That it might be fulfilled which was spoken by Isaiah the prophet, saying: "He Himself took our infirmities and bore our sicknesses."

There are teachers who say that the healing mentioned here is our new birth, our new spirit. Consider this: healing means to repair something to a previously good condition, to mend, to restore, to patch up. That cannot refer to our spirits. When we are born again our spirits are new. A new spiritual being is placed inside of us. The old one cannot be repaired. A new one is required, one that is perfect and clean so the Holy Spirit can live there and establish His abode as the Temple of God inside each one of us.

"For in Christ Jesus neither circumcision nor uncircumcision avails anything, but a new creation" (Galatians 6:15).

"Therefore, if anyone is in Christ, he is a new creation; old things have passed away; behold,

all things have become new" (2 Corinthians 5:17).

Now we can assess our own bodies and emotions and mental capacities and see that all those things are the same after salvation as they were before. The only thing that has become new is our spirit. That phenomenal force in our lives is brand new and looks and acts exactly like Jesus. Our job is to get our bodies and souls to behave like our spirits.

Jesus preached about the Kingdom of God wherever He went and He explicitly described its location. He kept saying it was at hand, it was at our fingertips. The Kingdom of Heaven is not far off some place, something yet to achieve; it is here and now for us to live in while we're on earth as well as when we get to heaven. Our eternal life began at the moment of our new birth.

> ***"Now when He was asked by the Pharisees when the kingdom of God would come, He answered them and said, "The kingdom of God does not come with observation; nor will they say, 'See here!' or 'See there!' For indeed, the kingdom of God is within you" (Luke 17:20-21).***

> ***"Jesus answered and said to him, "If anyone loves Me, he will keep My word; and My Father will love him, and We will come to Him and make Our home with him...." (John 14:23).***

*"And what agreement has the temple of God with
idols? For you are the temple of the living God.
As God has said: "I will dwell in them and walk
among them. I will be their God, and they shall
be My people" (2 Corinthians 6:16).*

God lives in His Kingdom and is in His temple all the
time. That Kingdom and that temple of the Kingdom
are in those of us who are born again! We simply have to
learn how to live there. We have to learn how to live with
healing because there is no sickness, disease, distress or
pain in the Kingdom of God where God lives and that
Kingdom is in us.

Apparently, there is something we have to do to obtain
this healing that Jesus paid such a price to give us, because
obviously we aren't healed. When I hold Healing Services
in churches about two-thirds of the people come forward
for prayer. The very people for whom Jesus died such an
excruciating death – are not healed.

John expresses a certain sense of responsibility that
belongs to the receiver of this great gift.

*"Beloved, I pray that you may prosper in all things and
be in health, just as your soul prospers" (3 John 1:2).*

Before we attack the subject of our responsibility, let us
make sure we fully accept that Jesus obtained healing for us

and that it now belongs to us. In fact, before God, because we are always before God since He lives in us, let us state our commitment to healing.

Please confess the following, that is, say it out loud.

Heavenly Father,

I am so grateful to be Your child and that You are my real Father.

Thank You for sending Jesus to redeem me from the enemy and give me a new birth.

Thank You that He is now my Lord and my Savior.

Thank You that Jesus' sacrifice before, on and after the cross obtained salvation for me and my sins are gone forever.

Thank You that His work purchased healing for my physical body and that healing belongs to me.

It is written in Matthew 8:17 that Jesus took my infirmities and He bore my sicknesses, which means that He carried on His body my sicknesses and diseases and I am healed.

It is written in 1 Peter 2:24 that by His stripes I was healed. If I was healed then I am healed.

I believe that in my heart and I say it with my mouth. Healing belongs to me and I am healed.

Amen!

Chapter 2

How to Obtain Healing

When I first moved to France as a missionary in 1988, I had no medical insurance, not in the United States nor in France. So when a mole on my left hand, being about the size of the pupil in the center of the iris of my eye, started growing, I ignored it because I didn't know what to do. Within a few weeks it grew to the size of the iris. It continued to grow, developed scaly rings around it and turned a dark, beet red.

A friend from the States came for a visit and I casually asked, "Do you think this is simply an age spot coming on me a bit early?"

Aghast, she responded gruffly, "That's cancer! You get to a doctor right away!"

I told her about my insurance problem and she told me she didn't care about my insurance problem, she was concerned with what looked to her like a lethal cancer and I better take care of it right away. Having shown her my abnormal tissue the day before she was leaving, I put her on the plane with promises to see a doctor immediately.

I went to see Doctor Jesus. Taking my Bible I looked up at least fifty Scriptures about healing. Now mind you, I had just graduated from Bible school and had memorized most of these very Scriptures, but I went through the process of looking them up. There is something about doing things methodically and meticulously that impresses our souls, at least it impresses mine.

First, I read the Scriptures to myself until I knew I was full. We know when we reach a state of fullness of the Word and in my opinion it is at this point that the Holy Spirit swings into action on our behalf. Of course, we never stay full of the Word; we seem to leak and we have to refill ourselves continually. But when I knew I was full I then read them out loud to the mole on my hand, which in my opinion had become unruly and rebellious!

Then I spoke to that mole from my heart. I said, "In the name of Jesus Christ of Nazareth, I curse you! I command you to get off my body now and never return!" Then I put my Bible away and went about my business.

The next morning when I woke up, before getting out of bed, I looked at the mole and the cancer and I said, "Thank God you're gone!" That's all. I got up and started my day singing away in the joy of the Lord.

The next morning when I woke up, I did exactly the same thing. It was all still there, unchanged, almost like a neon sign flashing in my eyes, but I wasn't going to be tripped up by appearances. I said emphatically as before, "Thank God you're gone!"

The next morning I went through the same ritual. On the fifth morning I woke up, pulled my hand up to once again speak to it and there was nothing to speak to. The cancer was gone and so was the mole without leaving even a tiny trace of what had been there all my life. Glory to God!

Now I am not holding myself up as some kind of successful Christian. I've had healing failures, which we will discuss later, but the failures have never been God's fault; they've all been mine. On this one, the success was complete, and so I use it as a demonstration.

What I did <u>not</u> do.

Please note what I did and what I did not do. I did not ask Jesus for healing. Why? He's already given it. I did not beg Him and plead with Him to give it to me. I knew I already had it because I am born again and my salvation includes healing. I did not allow my mind to go back and forth between 'yes, I have it' and 'no, I don't.' I did not diminish Jesus by disregarding what His painful victory on the cross accomplished for me; He didn't do that for Himself, He did it for me.

> *"For it pleased the Father that in Him all the fullness should dwell, and by Him to reconcile all things to Himself, by Him, whether things on earth or things in heaven, having made peace through the blood of His cross"* (Colossians 1:19-20).

I used His Word.

> *"My son, give attention to my words; incline your ear to my sayings. Do not let them depart from your eyes; keep them in the midst of your heart; for they are life to those who find them, and health to all their flesh"* (Proverbs 4:20-22).

The words which God has spoken bring health to all our flesh, and that is the Truth!

> *"Sanctify them by Your truth. Your word is truth"* (John 17:17).

We are the ones who use His Words on the earth. He has spoken them and they accomplish what He sent them to do when we speak them and believe them.

"Forever, O Lord, Your Word is settled in heaven" *(Psalm 119:89).*

"He sent His Word and healed them and delivered them from their destructions" (Psalm 107:20).

"I am watching to perform My Word" (Jeremiah 1:12).

"So shall My Word be that goes forth from My mouth; it shall not return to Me void, but it shall accomplish what I please, and it shall prosper in the thing for which I sent it" (Isaiah 55:11).

"Bless the Lord, you His angels, who excel in strength, who do His word, heeding the voice of His word" (Psalm 103:20).

Angels listen to what we say, we put voice to His Word, and they hear it and accomplish it for us. If we don't speak His Word, or speak words that agree with His Word, then we are not issuing orders to the angels. Note that we do not command angels; they serve God. He has appointed them to minister to us by the words that we speak which give voice to what He has already spoken.

"And the Word became flesh and dwelt among us, and we beheld His glory, the glory as of the only begotten of the Father, full of grace and truth" (John 1:14).

We know from this Scripture that Jesus is the Word. That may seem a little mystical to us, but then the Kingdom of God is mystical, so get over it. A mystic is simply someone who seeks spiritual truths and experiences. The only spiritual truth that exists is God and His Kingdom. The rest is a lie, a sham, a borrowed reality twisted to deceive and directed by Satan.

When we use the Word of God, we are using what Jesus achieved for us as it was foretold in the Old Testament and retold in the New Testament. That's why the Bible is our workbook, a book on how to live in the Kingdom of God. We take His Word, we apply it to our situations that exist in the natural world and they are forced to change. Look at how much importance God puts on His Word.

"For you have magnified Your Word above all our Name" (Psalm 138:2).

I used His Name.

"Our help is in the name of the Lord, who made heaven and earth" (Psalm 124:8).

I can just tell some of you want to get nitpicky with me. 'Yeah, but Marty, that Scripture talks about God, not Jesus.' Now let me get nitpicky with you. Jesus is God. God the Father, Jesus the Son and the Holy Spirit, the three in One make up God. Here's Jesus talking:

> *"And whatever you ask in My name, that I will do, that the Father may be glorified in the Son. If you ask anything in My name, I will do it" (John 14:13-14).*

> *"All things that the Father has are Mine. Therefore I said that He will take of Mine and declare it to you" (John 16:15).*

> *"Most assuredly, I say to you, whatever you ask the Father in My name He will give you. Until now you have asked nothing in My name. Ask, and you will receive, that your joy may be full" (John 16:23-24).*

These three Scriptures are all from the same 'sermon' Jesus gave just before going to the Garden of Gethsemane. Jesus is God. His name carries the same power today as He personally carried when He was here on the earth. For that power to be unleashed in our lives, we must believe what I just said: Jesus is God and His name carries the power and authority of God.

Today the simple name of Jesus has become quite familiar to us. He is, after all, our friend, our big brother,

the lover of our souls, our shepherd and our beloved, and
He definitely is all these things. At the same time that He is
so – everyday – to us, He is also our Master, our King, our
Redeemer, our Sure Foundation and our Commander, all
of which demand great respect and awe.

While I use the name of Jesus to be intimate and
confidential with Him, I use the fuller name to denote
His power and authority: Jesus Christ of Nazareth.
To me it's like the difference between a full name and
a nickname. The important thing is to know that the
name of Jesus carries with it the command of the throne
of God. Every demon knows this. They simply wait to
see if we know it.

> *"Therefore God also has highly exalted Him and
> given Him the name which is above every name that
> at the name of Jesus every knee should bow, of those
> in heaven and of those on earth, and of those under
> the earth, and that every tongue should confess
> that Jesus Christ is Lord, to the glory of God the
> Father" (Philippians 2:9-11).*

The name of Jesus merits our meditation. If angels,
people and demons know enough to bow their knees to
the name that is above all names, it seems to me that we
should give this subject a bit of study, to say the least.
In our mouths is our salvation with the profound word:
Jesus!

"And this is His commandment: that we should believe on the name of His Son Jesus Christ...." (1 John 3:23).

I used my faith.

"But without faith it is impossible to please God...." (Hebrews 11:6).

"...God has dealt to each one a measure of faith" (Romans 12:3).

What is faith, exactly? If we were to say that faith is believing that Jesus is the Son of God, then we'd have to say that the devil has faith because he believes that. The Bible calls our faith 'precious' and I don't think Satan has anything that is precious. The Scriptures tell us that we are each given a seed of faith when we're born again, so whatever we had beforehand is not the kind of faith the Bible is talking about. This faith is precious, a divine gift, and it accomplishes things.

The book of Romans has more to say about faith than any other book. Let's take a look at a few Scriptures in Romans in order to answer our question: What exactly is faith?

"For in it the righteousness of God is revealed from faith to faith; as it is written, "The just shall live by faith" (1:17).

3:22-26

22 Even the righteousness of God, through faith in Jesus Christ, to all and on all who believe. For there is no difference:

23 for all have sinned and fallen short of the glory of God,

24 being justified freely by His grace through the redemption that is in Christ Jesus,

25 whom God set forth as a propitiation by His blood, through faith, to demonstrate His righteousness, because in His forbearance God had passed over the sins that were previously committed,

26 to demonstrate at the present time His righteousness, that He might be just and the justifier of the one who has faith in Jesus.

14:23 *...for whatever is not from faith is sin.*

Let me attempt to put this in simple terms. Faith is something we live by because to live by anything else is sin. Our faith is in Jesus Christ for every aspect of life. Basically, we trust Jesus with everything: every decision, every purchase, every direction we take, everything we say, in other words, total trust. How far do we take this faith?

"Rejoice in the Lord always. Again I will say, rejoice! Let your gentleness be known to all men. The Lord is at hand. Be anxious for nothing, but in everything by prayer and supplication, with thanksgiving, let your requests be made known to God" (Philippians 4:4-6).

Sometimes I don't feel like rejoicing. Or giving thanks. But faith does that. Faith exerts itself to act appropriately. Faith rejoices when the mind can't see anything to rejoice about. Faith is gentle even though the emotions would like to knock somebody's lights out. Faith doesn't worry about a thing. Faith talks things over with the Lord and then completely trusts Him to take care of things. Once I spoke to that mole, I trusted God with all my heart to take the cancer away. There was no doubt in my mind.

"But let him ask in faith, with no doubting, for he who doubts is like a wave of the sea driven and tossed by the wind. For let not that man suppose that he will receive anything from the Lord: he is a double-minded man, unstable in all his ways" (James 1:6-8).

Some of the other times when I've needed healings, I've had doubts and just like this Scripture says, I received nothing. I'd wonder if I was going to get my healing this time; I'd doubt that I could have it, probably didn't deserve it and therefore God would withhold it. These attitudes are being double-minded. There is no faith in such thinking.

Obviously, I had faith in Jesus to take that mole and cancer away without harboring any doubts, and Jesus did take it away. So what is faith exactly? Absolute trust in Jesus Christ to take complete and total care of us. Does that sound difficult to achieve? The more we learn to live in the Kingdom of God right here, right now, the easier it becomes.

I spoke words.

First, I prepared my heart to believe. Then I used words to agree with my heart and I received what I believed. It works this way all the time.

> *"That if you confess with your mouth the Lord Jesus and believe in your heart that God has raised Him from the dead, you will be saved. For with the heart one believes unto righteousness, and with the mouth confession is made until salvation" (Romans 10:9-10).*

Look at this verse as if it is a safeguard, because it is. Two things must be in agreement for anything to happen in your life. You must believe in your heart and you must say with your mouth. Consider this: if you believe one thing and say another with your mouth, your faulty words will not accomplish what you said. But if you say what you believe, you will have it.

For salvation, we believed that Jesus died to save us and then we said it and so we had it. It never leaves because our salvation launched us into another realm. More about that later, right now let's look at the connection between beliefs and words.

If one day you're feeling spiteful and so you say, "Oh, Jesus doesn't love me. He didn't save me from anything." If you're born again, your heart knows better and so your status doesn't change. In fact after a few minutes, or maybe hours, or even days, your heart, which is so grieved by your words, will convict you to repent before God, probably in tears, and thank Him profusely for His salvation.

This is also how healing works. We believe in our hearts that we are healed and we confirm that belief with the words of our mouths. So little is known about Divine Healing. The global church has a tragic lack in pulpit and Sunday school teaching and therefore the Body of Christ, for the most part, doesn't have a conviction that healing belongs to them. They don't know their responsibility, which is to bring their hearts into revelation knowledge of healing and to make their words agree with the belief in their heart.

A woman in my church in Tours asked for prayer for a cold she was fighting and so I prayed for her and expected her to be healed. After the church service ended I heard her talking to a friend. "I am just so sick I don't know what to do! I can't stand the coughing and the sneezing and I'm so tired."

I stopped her and said, "I thought you believed in your healing."

"Oh, I do!" she retorted.

"No you don't. Listen to your words. You believe in your sickness."

Offended she asked, "What do I do? Pretend I'm not sick?"

"Never," I said. "Faith always acknowledges facts at the same time as proclaiming what it believes. Faith is constantly in the process of receiving."

"So what do I say?"

"Well, you figure it out. Try speaking faith right now."

"Okay. Let's see, I'm tired of the coughing and the sneezing so I'm really glad these symptoms are leaving me now because by His stripes I am healed."

"Good for you! Was that so hard?"

"No!" she laughed. "In fact, I feel better already."

This woman's heart believed or she wouldn't have come for prayer. But her head obviously disagreed and her words were in agreement with what her head believed and so healing was impossible until she changed her ways.

The whole world will agree with your sickness. Look at the television ads when fall begins. "Do you have sneezing, coughing, flu-like symptoms? Try...." They convince you, don't they, that you, indeed, are sick and need their medication, even though it really does little for you. We have to choose which side we're on! The world's side? Or God's?

Let's establish our faith in our healing by saying out loud the following:

Jesus, thank You for giving me Your Word.
I will study Your Word to discover the promises You have made
to me.
I will believe Your Word and I will use Your Word.
I will speak Your Word out loud and cover every situation in
my life with Your life-giving Word.
I will live by Your Word.
Thank You for giving me Your Name.
I will honor and bless Your Name.
I will study Your Name in Your Word so that I can
comprehend everything that is contained in Your Name.
I will praise Your Name and magnify Your Name when I talk
about it.
I will use Your Name to apply Your power and authority on
this earth.
Thank You for giving me a seed of faith.
I will use my faith as an active ingredient in my life.
I will value my faith and make it grow.
I will apply my faith to every problem I have in life and I will
see the solution manifest.
Thank You for being the only trustworthy one in whom I have
complete confidence.
I will speak my faith.
I will use my words to proclaim Your Glory, Your Promises,
Your Goodness.
Thank You for giving me tools to use.
You, the Great I Am, are my God, my King, my Healer, my
Savior and my God Omnipotent!
Amen.

Chapter 3

Current Mentality About Healing

During the three years I attended Bible school, I also acted as a Prayer Partner for the hospital built by Oral Roberts called City of Faith. After school I went to the hospital and picked up the list of patients that had been assigned to me for that day. Then I went to each patient, knocked on the door, stuck my head into the room saying, "I'm a Prayer Partner. Would you like for me to pray for you?"

No one ever said 'No.' I listened to their prayer requests and then I would pray, being careful to be guided by the Holy Spirit in what I said. I saw the Lord perform so many magnificent healings and miracles that I could write reams about these experiences.

That hospital was phenomenal. Not only did a Prayer Partner pray, but everyone who entered the room asked if they could pray. Even the people who cleaned the rooms! The clerical staff! Everybody prayed! If a hospital could be said to be heaven on earth, in my opinion that one could.

Unfortunately, the lack of finances caused it to be closed, but the blessing that went along with the closing sent prayer into other hospitals all over the United States. The medical personnel took the concept wherever they went.

One day I got on the elevator on my way to see my next patient and in the elevator was a woman on a gurney and a nurse taking her to surgery. Normally a patient on the way to the surgical theatre is pretty dopey having already received strong medication to prepare them for the operation. However, this woman was still quite awake and she had been crying. The nurse looked despondent so I asked if I could pray.

They responded as if they knew the problem was hopeless. A variety of nurses and doctors had tried to put a needle in the woman's arm to anesthetize her. No one got the needle in because they couldn't find a vein. She had been poked dozens of times. The woman had plump arms with the kind of creamy skin that never seems to show a black and blue mark.

I looked the woman in the eyes and told her to be in agreement with me. She nodded. I put my hand on her arm and in the name of Jesus I commanded a vein to come to the surface and stay there throughout the surgery. When I lifted my hand a nice strong vein stood right under the skin all the way down her arm. The elevator door opened on my floor and I left.

Later in the day I saw the nurse again. She elatedly told me the needle went right into the vein; the woman fell asleep and successfully endured the operation. Looking at me quizzically she said, "That prayer you did was very strange. I didn't feel one bit of that special anointing, and yet the vein showed up."

I said, "I didn't need a special anointing because I was using the authority of Jesus and I was using my faith." She looked at me as if I had just landed from another planet and I realized she had no understanding of what I said.

The nurse's reaction leads me into explaining another means of being healed and it also demonstrates the current mentality in the church about healing. Personally, I describe the current mentality as a lack of responsibility, but before I go into that, let me give you another avenue to receive your healing.

In 1 Corinthians 12 Paul discusses some activities of the Holy Spirit. He says the Holy Spirit has gifts to disperse, one of which he calls "gifts of healings." Then he says in verse 11,

> **But one and the same Spirit works all these things (the gifts), distributing to each one individually as**

He wills.

Notice that "gifts of healings" is in the plural. Generally speaking, it's the evangelists who carry these healing gifts and you don't have to be around them too long to realize that each evangelist has a slightly different healing anointing. One may have more success in restoring sight, another in restoring hearing, or someone might have an anointing for healing abdominal organs, or for broken bones. It's as the Spirit wills.

There is an anointing to these gifts that comes and goes. In a public meeting where the evangelist has prepared him or herself, a tangible anointing can be felt. But the next day when the evangelist strolls through a shopping mall and someone stops him or her for prayer, usually the anointing is not present and nothing will happen.

As a young Christian I observed an elderly and obviously experienced man pray for people with bad backs. I didn't have a bad back, but I could clearly see that those who did were instantly helped as they danced away with joy and no more pain.

I waited till everyone left and then I asked the man if he would pray for my hands that I could also pray for people with bad backs. When he laid his hands on mine to pray, from my fingertips to my elbows my skin turned bright red. He told me I had been given an anointing to pray for the sick and to never hesitate to respond to a request for prayer.

The very next day someone asked me to pray for a man who had been bent forward from the waist for eleven years. I balked at the idea; surely I should start with a simple backache or something easy. However, I remembered the gentleman's instructions about not hesitating, so I stepped up to the man and prayed.

Laying my hands on his spine, the heel of one hand on his waist, my fingers pointing upward, the heel of the other hand touching the tips of my fingers and thereby covering as much of his curving spine as I could, I commanded his back, in the name of Jesus, to be healed and to straighten up. I often find myself using words from Psalm 139, "The Bible says you are perfect and wonderfully made, now be perfect and wonderfully made."

As I was thanking God for His healing power given to this man, he stood upright. I saw him again three days later, standing straight as an arrow, grinning ear to ear and he gave me a big bear hug right there on the street! He said, "I haven't been able to hug anybody for eleven years!"

Just because I have this particular gift of healing, which operates as the Holy Spirit wills, doesn't mean I can't pray for other things and have success. Obviously, I can use my faith on any healing. But whether my prayer is based on the gift of healing in the presence of the Holy Spirit or on my faith in what

Jesus did for us on the cross, I must put myself into complete subjection to Him for healing to operate through me,

There are other references for having an intermediary pray.

> *"…they will lay hands on the sick, and they will recover" (Mark 16:18).*

> *"Is anyone among you sick? Let him call for the elders of the church, and let them pray over him anointing him with oil in the name of the Lord. And the prayer of faith will save the sick and the Lord will raise him up" (James 5:14-15).*

Often the purpose of having a third party pray, like an evangelist, is to demonstrate signs and wonders to the unsaved and bring them to Christ. Paul, in speaking of his own ministry as a traveling evangelist as well as being an apostle, says,

> *"For I will not dare to speak of any of those things which Christ has not accomplished through me, in word and deed, to make the Gentiles obedient – in mighty signs and wonders, by the power of the Spirit of God, so that from Jerusalem and round about to Illyricum I have fully preached the gospel of Christ" (Romans 15:18-19).*

Paul says his ministry demonstrated signs and wonders by the power of the Spirit of God so that the Gentiles would receive Jesus as their Lord and become obedient to the gospel of Christ. That's one purpose of the power of the Holy Spirit—to do signs and wonders. There's very little evidence that signs and wonders are given to evangelists for Christians to be healed. In fact, the amount of Scripture pointing to healing for Christians being obtained by faith outweighs healing obtained by the anointing at least ten to one.

I like the fact that Paul says he won't speak of anything that happens outside of what the Holy Spirit does. Evangelists are often such buoyant, enthusiastic people that they are accused of exaggerating when they tell of their exploits. I understand that because I have received such criticism. It's not that the evangelist wants to 'blow his own horn,' it's that the event was so exciting he wants the listener to capture the thrill of what God did.

There is definitely an anointing that comes on these evangelists. Sometimes it feels like being put into a gelatinous egg and you know that no one but Jesus Christ is doing this work because you feel like you can't move on your own. Sometimes it feels so natural, so ordinary that it is only when it's over and the anointing lifts that you realize you were taken over by the Holy Spirit of God.

One time while praying before a healing service, the Lord told me that there would be 100% healings that night. It was at this precise moment that the anointing filled me, but it was only when I looked back to analyze the event that I realized when the anointing began. My response to this divine announcement was simply, "Oh. Good." No big deal. Of course. Even though I've never known anybody to have 100% healings in a service, the anointing brought with it an unconditional acceptance of what God wanted.

In that service I prayed for dozens of people who remarkably had ills that could be easily seen like swollen joints or a limp or a growth and easily noted when they were healed. Just like the Lord said, 100% of them were healed. It got so that people would stand up to watch. They moved closer to crowd into the front pews.

Then just before closing the service I asked if anyone had scoliosis. Scoliosis is a condition of the spine that makes it curve into an S shape and it severely limits the person's activities. The entire church turned to look at one of their teenagers and she shyly raised her hand. I invited her up front like we were old friends and she came.

She was wearing a t-shirt, it being summer, so I asked her to bend over so that I could see the outline of her spine. When she did I had the audacity to ask the audience if they could also see it and I asked several women to come up and trace the outline with their fingers. It was a severe curvature and the women gasped as they ran their fingers down her spine. Then I asked them to stay and watch her spine straighten up while I prayed.

Trust me. I am bold, but I'm not this bold. I had never done anything like this in a service in my life! But under the anointing it seemed so natural! Then I laid my hands on her spine. The women jumped back and people in the audience exclaimed because the bones could be heard making cracking sounds as they moved. When I removed my hands her spine was perfectly straight as the women could testify. She stood up and started running around the church. Her family and friends were jumping, clapping and crying for joy!

She came rushing back to me and asked if she could call her girlfriend because the girlfriend had scoliosis worse than she had had. I said it's the end of the service. Everyone wants to go home. But she begged and begged so I said okay. If she could be here in ten minutes I'd pray. Off she ran to the telephone and I dismissed the people.

Normally the anointing starts to fade at this point; that's why I was hesitant. However, I wasn't really aware of the anointing because I have to say it again, it was so natural. The girl came in with her friend when the sanctuary was just about empty. This particular teenager had such bad scoliosis that she could not lift her foot to climb a stair. If she did she would faint.

Since we were about the only ones left I had this new girl bend over while the already healed girl acted as witness. She traced the line of the spine, I laid hands on the girl's back, just like I had done with the first one, said pretty much the same words as I said before and commanded her back to straighten up. Again, we could hear the bones making a cracking noise as they moved, perhaps even louder and harder than the first girl.

When I removed my hands her spine was perfectly straight. She said, "I need to see for myself," and she headed right for the stairs leading up to the platform. She climbed up and ran back down. The look on her face was priceless. She just kept going up and down. People came back in from the parking lot to watch as she must have gone up and down those four steps a hundred times, totally healed, squealing out her joy.

The Pastor stood by the door as the people exited and so he met me in the parking lot when I came out of the church, the last to leave. He said, "I won't be inviting you back to this church again. What you did tonight was too charismatic for us." That was the moment the anointing lifted and I realized I was being put through a test. Jesus had done great things that night, so how would I receive this rebuke.

Fortunately, I won that battle. I said, "I'm so sorry to have offended you. Please forgive me. Thank you so much for allowing me to speak tonight. You have a wonderful church."

When the anointing lifts I am either so tired I can barely crawl home or I am so jazzed up I can't get to sleep for hours afterward. That night I was exhausted so I excused myself, waved to the few people still talking in the parking lot, and drove home.

Four months later I heard that Pastor was fired. I can only imagine what happened in that period of time between the members who now thoroughly believed in healing and those who didn't. Faith in healing is a volatile subject. It does divide churches. I personally never want what I believe to divide me from Christ. The Bible has to be my only measuring tape and I look for the day that the Bible, and the whole teaching therein, is the Church's only measuring tape. Experience is never stronger than the Word; just because somebody you know didn't receive their healing, that does not make the Word wrong. Failed healings are never stronger than the Word of God.

Let's get back to our discussion about faith for healing. Even in James 5:14-15, which we read earlier and find to be a Scripture directed toward believers, the emphasis is on faith. It says to call for the elders. Elders are mature Christians and you will recognize a mature Christian by the way they pray. They don't beg, plead or try to wheedle things out of God; they pray according to faith. They don't cry and whine; they praise God for what He has already given and they take authority over the disease.

> *"I write to you, fathers, because you have known Him who is from the beginning" (1 John 2:13).*

Elders are the fathers in the faith because they have spent time getting to know God and that can't be done without first getting to know His Word. If you want results, find someone who knows God to pray for you, not someone who knows about God. As James 5:15 says, it is the prayer of faith that saves the sick. It doesn't matter who is doing the praying, you or the intermediary, nothing will happen without faith.

I believe any Christian is capable of praying for someone else's healing and all of us should step right up and offer to pray when we see someone in need. I learned first hand how important other Christian's prayers can be! One night I jumped into my car and as I shifted into drive I felt something sting my middle finger on the gear shift. Living in Florida at the time I thought nothing of it. A mosquito, no doubt.

It was a busy time for me. As Pastor of a Church I planned a revival which started in two days and I was roaring off on errands. Though the pain of the sting did not subside, I paid no attention to it. No time.

By the following morning the location of the sting on my middle finger had turned black and created a hole in my skin but no big deal. I went on about my hectic schedule. That night as I ironed my dress for the next morning's first meeting my phone rang. A good friend of mine said, "Marty, the Lord is telling me to come get you and take you to the hospital. What's wrong?"

Instinctively I looked at the mark of the sting. Red lines coming from that place were working their way up my forearm and some had reached my elbow. When I described that to her she said, "I'll be right over!"

"Don't do that. It's ten o'clock at night! I've got a revival starting tomorrow. I can't afford to go to the hospital; who will take care of things for me?"

She hung up without hearing me and was at my door in an amazing ten minutes. She unplugged my iron, grabbed my purse and literally pushed me all the way to her car. The personnel in the emergency room agreed instantly that I had been bitten by a Brown Recluse Spider, one of the most fatal spider bites in the world. They told me they would have to amputate my arm right away to prevent the poison from reaching my heart. If they didn't amputate, I would die within 24 hours, or less, depending on how fast the poison traveled.

Betty and I looked at each other in shock and then as if we had planned it, turned to the personnel and said in unison, "No!" My friend prayed on the spot commanding that poison to stop right that second and to die and dissipate in my body.

Dumbfounded, the personnel said they had to keep me overnight, at least, to monitor the progress. I threw up my hands, wondering what about my poor revival, and surrendered. Okay. Betty, of course, took care of everything. She went home and called every prayer group she could think of, even if it was midnight!

The nurse came into my room and gave me a steroid shot saying it was the least they could do. All night they checked on me every hour and every hour the red lines had receded a little bit more. By morning they were gone and by the afternoon all that remained was a tiny little scar where the spider had bitten me. It's still there reminding me of the goodness of God and the faithfulness of my brothers and sisters in Christ. Thank God for Christians who listen to the voice of God and obey and who know how to pray! That evening I sat in my own church like a member attending the revival. Betty had it well in hand.

Now let's go back to the nurse in my story about the City of Faith. She was looking for the power of the Holy Spirit to supply the results they wanted in the woman's arm. Without that anointing she didn't think it was possible for anything to happen.

That's where the church is today, chasing after anointings. They move like a swarm from one big meeting to another, and they're so disappointed when they go home and they're not healed. They don't recognize that it's the prayer of faith that heals the sick Christian.

That prayer of faith takes responsibility. It takes making a determined decision that you ARE going to receive your healing because you KNOW Jesus paid such a horrific price for it. It means applying the Word and applying the Name. It means exercising your faith, even when you don't feel like it.

Is the church lazy? Maybe. Is the church misinformed? Many are. Does the church want somebody else to do the work? For the most part, yes. A Christian can wait around until an anointing happens to fall on them, or a Christian can take the purchase price of the stripes of Jesus that bought their healing for them and appropriate the awesome gift of healing that He gave. Appropriating healing is part of the work required of a Christian. After all, the only fight a Christian fights is the fight of faith.

Christians need to learn to be honest about the level of their faith. Over all my years in the Body of Christ I have seen that absolutely no one is at the same level of faith as anyone else. We are all growing in different measures.

Twice I was a patient in the City of Faith. The first time I went in I had a hysterectomy. This happened right at the beginning of Bible school so I was surrounded by students thumping me on the back and telling me not to get the operation but to grab my healing by faith! Yes! Amen!

But in the dark of the night, lying awake on my bed, I knew I didn't have the faith for that. I asked the Lord what to do. He told me to do whatever the doctor said. When I went to the doctor, and he was a Christian, he asked me what I wanted as I could live with the problem until I went through the 'change.' With my family's history that would be another ten years, at least. I said, "You see hundreds of women. I only know myself. What do you suggest?"

He said, "Get the hysterectomy and get it over with. You'll be much happier." So now I had direction. I would get the operation.

In my satisfaction over this decision, the Lord asked me a puzzling question. "What do you have faith for?"

I thought and thought and finally answered. "I can have faith for no pain."

When it was all over and I realized what I had done, I marveled. After all, abdominal surgery, yes they did cut me open from side to side, is one of the most painful surgeries around. But I blissfully stepped into a state of faith for no pain. After the operation, after the recovery room, after 5 or 6 hours of sleep, a nurse woke me up.

"It's been nine hours since you came off the operating table and you haven't asked for any pain medication. What's wrong? What can we do for you?"

For a minute I analyzed how I felt and I shrugged and said, "I don't have any pain. Don't give me any medication. I don't want it."

She patted me on the shoulder and said, "Well, if you change your mind, let us know."

I never took one pill. The prescription they sent home with me sat on my shelf for years till I finally threw it out. But accomplishing that step of faith fortified me so much! I knew how much faith I had and I used it. It's important to be honest about what you can believe for. That experience is what made me want to be a Prayer Partner.

My second operation came at the end of Bible school. Right out of college I taught Physical Education and developed bunions by wearing bad tennis shoes and walking, running, etc. on hard surfaces. Now, 20+ years later, the bunions dominated my feet. I could stand for about an hour but after that, forget it!

All during Bible school I worked on my faith to get those bunions off my feet. But to no avail, so I chose surgery. I was headed for the mission field and I needed good feet to carry the Gospel of Jesus Christ. This time I asked myself what I could believe for and decided to once again go for no pain, but also a quick recovery. I wanted to be back on my feet in three weeks. With the kind of surgery I had the doctor told me it would take about nine weeks before I could walk and then I would be shaky.

My faith worked perfectly. I spent three weeks in a wheelchair with my feet encased in those clumsy boots, but then three weeks to the day I took those boots off and discarded the wheelchair and I walked strong the minute I stood on my own. I am so grateful for that operation. Today I can walk for hours without ever feeling the effects in my feet.

God is the author of medicine and medical personnel. He sent us that help. It's okay for a Christian to use doctors and combine faith with whatever they do. They know they're not the healer and we know it's Jesus who is the Healer. I don't go to the doctor often, but I'm glad to go because I count on them to give me the name of what I am fighting. Then I can use my faith against whatever is attacking me.

For instance, last year I suffered from extreme fatigue and what appeared to be deep bronchitis. I went to the doctor. After myriads of tests I was told I had developed air-borne allergies. They told me what kind of over the counter drugs to use, gave me a steroid shot and told me to come back once a year for that same shot.

I followed the advice for about a week and then I thought, "What on earth am I doing? I know better! No weapon formed against me will ever prosper!" I began commanding allergies to leave my body even though I didn't know exactly what allergies I had! When I knew I was full of the Word, which meant my faith was built up, I stopped taking the medication because I was just fine.

About six months ago after weeks of rain, the same conditions came on me again. The Holy Spirit directed me to look around the edges of the window in my bedroom and there I discovered mold. Now I knew where the air-borne allergy came from. I cleaned up the mold and commanded those spores to leave me alone and commanded my body to be healthy. The conditions instantly disappeared. Many of my friends have mold allergies and when I told them the symptoms were gone they wouldn't believe me. "Impossible!" they would say because they've gone through the misery of that affliction. Months later they are still asking me, "How's the mold?" I just smile and shake my head.

But healing by faith is possible. In fact it is the way Jesus wants us to be healed. Yes, there is an anointing to attract the unsaved but the healing God provides for His children is through the stripes of Jesus.

Waiting for the anointing to heal is like the man who lay by the pool of Bethesda for 38 years waiting for healing.

An angel occasionally came and stirred the water and the first one to enter the water would be healed. This man had never made it into the water! So there he lay.

Christians may not be lying by the water, but waiting on someone else's anointing in order to grab a healing seems very similar to me. Especially when healing belongs to us. Jesus acquired it on our behalf. He doesn't need healing; we do.

Jesus asked that man, "Do you want to be made well?"

Why don't we ask ourselves the same question? I should think that anyone in their right mind wants healing, but I have also learned along the way that there are those who don't want healing. The first time I ran into this dilemma a certain woman had invited me to her home to pray for her arms. She couldn't lift them above her head.

I laid my hands on her shoulders covering the joints and I could feel the healing anointing run down my arms into her shoulders. All of a sudden that anointing came rushing back into my arms and practically pulled them out of my own shoulder sockets. I asked her if she really wanted to be healed and she admitted to me, "No."

I asked why not and she said if she were healed she would lose her disability check and have to go back to work. She had a deep, deep fear left over from the severe poverty in her childhood of not having any money. Her faulty shoulder joints kept money coming into her account and she'd rather have the money than her health. Brothers and sisters in Christ, don't nag people who prefer being sick; love them. It is something lurking in their subconscious that causes them to feel this way.

If you, however, want your God-given healing, then take it! Take it by faith! It's yours! It belongs to you! Don't go along with the crowd that flocks to hear every visiting preacher in hopes of maybe receiving healing, something, maybe receiving a word, anything, when you can have it all by faith.

What we should be doing with these visiting evangelists is taking our unsaved friends to hear them preach so they can experience the signs and wonders. Maybe another question I should ask is this: Is the church selfish? I'll let you answer that one. For myself I describe the Church today and its current mentality on healing as being: immature. John gives us three stages of growth: little children, young men and fathers.

> *"I write to you, little children, because your sins are forgiven you for His name's sake. I write to you, fathers, because you have known Him who is from the beginning. I write to you, young men, because you have overcome the wicked one" (1 John 2:12-13).*

It's the babies who chase after anointings; the adults know how to overcome Satan and they know Jesus so they turn to the Lord. Commit yourself to a deeper Christian experience.

"That the God of our Lord Jesus Christ, the Father of glory, may give to you the spirit of wisdom and revelation in the knowledge of Him" (Ephesians 1:17).

Knowing Him. That is the pinnacle of the Christian experience.   Having Him reveal Himself, manifest Himself to us, brings the spirit of wisdom.   May we all be filled with the knowledge of His will in all wisdom and spiritual understanding.   May we know Him as we are known by Him.

Please say the following from your heart in an out loud voice:

Father, teach me how to overcome the wicked one.

Please teach me all about You. I want to know You.

I want to grow up into the fullness of a man or woman of God.

I will study Your Word about healing. Please give me revelation knowledge about this magnificent gift Jesus gave me.

Amen.

Chapter 4

Why Some People Aren't Healed and/or Why Some People Lose their Healing

In my first year as a missionary in France I noticed that my left ear didn't hear as sharply as it did before. The difference was very slight, but it bothered me. I was too young for the loss of hearing that occurs in the decline of life.

If you've ever watched a dog with a thistle in its ear then you know what I went through. That dog will shake its head, scratch that ear, rub it on the ground, anything to get that thistle out of its ear. I cleaned, I de-waxed, I poured in warm oil, anything to get that hearing back up to par. Even my darling daughter helped me with these tasks. Nothing worked.

Finally, I went on a round of Ear, Nose and Throat Specialists, quitting after the third doctor in a row said he didn't know why my hearing was failing. The loss wasn't bad enough for a hearing aid so they could do nothing for me.

Twenty years later I don't hear anything in that ear and medical science now has an answer for it. A growth of bony tissue overgrew the little stirrup bone and ossified it. This summer I will have the operation that will scrape away those overzealous cells and replace that tiny bone with a stainless steel pendulum which will restore my hearing.

About twelve years ago I happened to be in the States sitting in an audience listening to one of my favorite, and in my mind, highly respected ministers of God. After speaking he began calling out ailments and asking the people to come forward for healing at which point he laid hands on them and commanded the sickness to leave, in the name of Jesus.

I had not attended the meeting for this purpose because I knew I was supposed to receive my healing by faith, even though my attempts had been half-hearted in the case of my ear. However, I reflected. "Lord, if you want to use this occasion to heal my ear, then have him call out exactly 'deafness in the left ear.'"

That was the very next thing he called. "Someone in here suffers from deafness in the left ear. If that's you, please raise your hand."

There were probably 1000 people in that meeting and not one person raised their hand. I thought, 'Surely there is somebody else!' But no. He continued to call. "I know what the Lord said and I am not moving on until that person is healed. Who is it?" He doggedly persisted in calling for deafness in the left ear.

With great timidity I raised my hand barely above my head. Of course the whole audience is now looking for this person and they all point at me as he had come down to the floor to walk among the rows of people hunting for the one with deafness in the left ear.

He invited me to join him at the center of the floor which I did. Everyone, still as a mouse, intently watched to see a miracle. Every step I took resounded in the silent hall. He didn't say a word to me; he put one hand on top of my head and one hand on my left ear. I felt like my head had been captured in a vise!

"COME OUT OF HER!" he commanded. He rebuked the spirit of infirmity and the deaf and dumb spirit and then suddenly pulled his hands away like retrieving them from a fire. I felt nothing during this time except that when he let go my head was released from that vise! He ordered me to plug my right ear with a finger, which I did, and then he asked if I could hear him.

Marveling, I said yes I could. When I came to the center of the floor my left ear could only hear sounds, not distinct words. Now I heard distinct words, not at normal volume, but they were there.

He walked about twenty feet away and asked again if I could hear him. Yes, I could! Then he had me turn away from him and he said something different. Could I still hear him? Yes, I could! I explained that even though the words were distinct, they were low volume.

He clarified my concerns saying that the Bible says we shall lay hands on the sick and they will recover which indicates a time period for recuperation. In other words, be patient. The fullness of volume would happen. I returned to my chair amid applause and people extending their hands to congratulate me by shaking my hand.

I listened to the rest of his ministry with my finger in my right ear so that I could only use my left ear to hear. When the meeting ended I went straight to my car, no longer keeping my finger in my right ear because I needed the use of my right hand. As I unlocked my car I heard two women by the next car talking about the meeting.

With a little smile on my face I put my finger in my right ear to listen to them with my left ear and I heard nothing. I kept listening to the hum of the void of sound and my smile turned to a frown. Sighing deeply I muttered within myself, "I guess I didn't receive my healing after all."

In the Bible there is only one reason for someone not receiving their healing: Unbelief. That is also the only reason for someone losing their healing: Unbelief. When Jesus traveled to his own part of the country where the people had known Him as a child, they did not receive His ministry of teaching and healing. After all, He'd been a kid running around their village. Who did He think He was?

> ***"Now He did not do many mighty works there because of their unbelief" (Matthew 13:58).***

Mark's version of this same story puts it into more concrete action.

> ***"Now He could do no mighty work there, except that He laid His hands on a few sick people and healed them" (Mark 6:6).***

Jesus took Peter, James and John up a mountain which we call the Mount of Transfiguration because the three disciples saw Jesus transfigured until His face shone like the sun and His clothes became white as light. The other disciples remained at the bottom of the mountain and ministered to the people.

When Jesus and the three came off the mountain a certain man asked Jesus to cure his son of epilepsy as the disciples had been unable to help. Jesus rebuked the demon and the epilepsy left the child. The disciples asked why they had not been able to cast the demon out.

*"So Jesus said to them, "Because of your unbelief,
for assuredly, I say to you, if you have faith as a
mustard seed, you will say to this mountain, 'Move
from here to there,' and it will move; and nothing
will be impossible for you" (Matthew 17:20).*

What I said to myself by my car, was that a statement
of faith or unbelief? Obviously, unbelief. You might say,
"But Marty, God understands." Of course He understands,
however, that doesn't make it right. I understood when my
children played in the mud in their good, clean, ready to go
to church clothes. It was fun. But that didn't make it right.
They still got a spanking.

You might say, 'Isn't that a little harsh? I mean, one little
statement in the middle of the night.... Come on!'

Consider what God did for me. He brought me back to
the States at that precise time. He took me to a meeting with
one of the few men (or women) who will hear from God in
front of a thousand people and then refuse to continue until
he can accomplish what God wants, even if he looks foolish
wandering around the sanctuary, hunting. And then I am
the only person in the whole crowd with deafness in the
left ear? He kept everyone else away! We know that many
people have some kind of hearing distress due to the boom
boxes and the ear phones and the loud speakers we have
been using for decades. And I say, "I guess I didn't get my
healing after all."

Paul, in talking about Abraham, says this:

"He did not waver at the promise of God through unbelief, but was strengthened in faith, giving glory to God" (Romans 4:20).

Abraham didn't waver like I did. I should have called upon my faith like Abraham did. I should have given glory to God. Sometimes the word "unbelief" is translated "disobedience;" that's just how severe unbelief is.

Hebrews chapters 3 and 4 discuss the Rest that God has provided, the Sabbath of the New Testament. In the Old Testament the Sabbath meant one day a week for physical rest which for us today is a type and shadow of what Jesus provided. There is a Rest we enter into when we are born again and that Sabbath is designed to give us peace and rest 24 hours a day. We enter into complete and total trust that God is taking care of it, no matter what 'it' is. If we don't enter this Rest it is because of our unbelief and our unbelief is considered to be disobedience.

That's serious stuff. God demonstrated this Rest by Himself resting on the seventh day.

"There remains therefore a rest for the people of God. For he who has entered His rest has himself also ceased from his works as God did from His" (Hebrews 4:9-10).

We enter God's Rest by ceasing from our works. This does not refer to physical labor or mental labor, it refers to making things happen. It refers to carrying the weight of unbelief instead of the total freedom of trust in God. 'Our works' means trusting in ourselves instead of trusting in God.

God is not a tyrant. He doesn't hit us over the head with a two by four when we fall short, when we do our own works or when we let our faith walk fall by the wayside. He waits. When I finally realized the error I had made with the healing I received for my left ear, having so lightly tossed it away with my unbelief, I repented and He was right there waiting for me. At that moment I felt something in my right ear and from that time on my right ear heard well enough for two ears.

My doctor tells me that my left ear, which will be operated on in a few months, has perfect hearing underneath the extra cells freezing my stirrup bone. My right ear is showing signs of aging effects, though not enough for a hearing aid, and after the operation my left ear will be able to hear and compensate for my right one.

"For we know that all things work together for good to those who love God, to those who are the called according to His purpose" (Romans 8:28).

There's another reason Christians don't receive their healing, or they lose their healing, and that is found in Paul's writings also.

"Therefore whoever eats this bread or drinks this cup of the Lord in an unworthy manner will be guilty of the body and the blood of the Lord. But let a man examine himself, and so let him eat of the bread and drink of the cup. For he who eats and drinks in an unworthy manner eats and drinks judgment to himself, not discerning the Lord's body. For this reason many are weak and sick among you, and many are dead" (1 Corinthians 11:27-30).

I think this may be one of the topmost sins the Church makes. It's not that we take the Blood lightly; it's that we don't take it seriously enough. I've only been in one church that took the Blood lightly. All the rest I believe are truly sincere, they just aren't sincere enough.

In that particular church in the middle of the service they gave each person about four ounces of grape juice and a cupcake and everyone strolled around the sanctuary enjoying their snack while they socialized for 15 minutes. Then they sat back down and carried on.

I understand what they were doing. They interpreted these passages to mean they were not discerning the Body, or Christians collectively, so they were wanting personal contact. Let's let the Bible interpret itself on this subject.

"I am the living bread which came down from heaven. If anyone eats of this bread, he will live forever and the bread that I shall give is My flesh,

which I shall give for the life of the world" (John 6:51).

"By that will we have been sanctified (set apart) through the offering of the body of Jesus Christ once for all" (Hebrews 10:10).

"Of how much worse punishment, do you suppose, will he be thought worthy who has trampled the Son of God underfoot, counted the blood of the covenant by which he was sanctified a common thing, and insulted the Spirit of grace?" (Hebrews 10:29).

"Examine yourselves as to whether you are in the faith. Test yourselves. Do you not know yourselves, that Jesus Christ is in you?" (2 Corinthians 13:5).

From what I read I perceive that taking the Body and the Blood of Jesus Christ lightly, taking the Kingdom of God lightly, taking the indwelling of God lightly is what brings us to weakness, sickness and death. Do you know why Jesus sweat blood in the Garden of Gethsemane the night before He died? He knew what awaited Him.

When the man with the whip expertly flayed the body of Jesus, after all, it was the man's profession and I'm sure he practiced day and night to be precise each time he laid the whip on a human's hide, Jesus received more than a torturous beating. He received all the sins of mankind. He received all the sicknesses and diseases, distresses and pains that Satan had inflicted on humanity.

"Yet it pleased the Lord to crush Him; He has put Him to pain..." (Isaiah 53:10).

It goes on to say that God made the soul of Jesus an offering for sin. He who knew no sin carried our sins on His body. In heaven the four living creatures and the 24 elders sang this song:

"You are worthy to take the scroll, and to open its seals; for You were slain, and have redeemed us to God by Your blood out of every tribe and tongue and people and nation, and have made us kings and priests to our God and we shall reign on the earth" (Revelation 5:9-10).

Jesus paid the price for all mankind. It's paid for. There's nothing left to work for as He paid for it all. His blood even turned us into kings and priests and set us up to reign on the earth. He did it! We receive it! We open ourselves up and receive all this work He did before, on and after the cross.

When I take communion I can get very excited over what He did for me! He took my failures! He took my weaknesses! He took my poverty! He was chastised for my Shalom: my peace, my prosperity!

This may seem like a silly analogy, but I once had a friend who would put a biscuit on his dog's nose. The dog simply sat there looking cross-eyed at the biscuit until his master said, "It's paid for." Then the dog would toss the cookie in the air, catch it and eat it.

Our SALVATION (yes, I am shouting the word because it is so great a gift!) has been paid for, but for us to partake we must take of it. We must take the eternal life; we must take the forgiveness of sins; we must take the healing; we must take the Kingdom of God; we must take the indwelling Christ and we must not take all of that lightly. The gift was too profound to lightly dismiss. "It's paid for!"

I much prefer taking communion at home because there I can give it the attention it deserves. The Lord and I can share a most intimate moment as I adore Him to the very best of my ability and He can pour out His love on me for appreciating His gift. I sometimes marvel at what a shoddy substitute that piece of bread is for the battered body of Jesus Christ. Likewise, the cup of juice or wine, what a poor replacement for a cup of blood.

Some churches take communion as a ritual, but it's not. It's an honoring. It's a remembering of exactly what that Body and that Blood accomplished for us. It's a time of determining to receive with grace what was given by Grace.

"And when He had given thanks, He broke it and said, "Take, eat; this is My body which is broken for you; do this in remembrance of Me." In the same manner He also took the cup after supper, saying,

"This cup is the new covenant in My blood. This do, as often as you drink it, in remembrance of Me" (1 Corinthians 11:24-25).

How often are we to take communion? As often as we want. If I had a terminal disease I'd probably take it every hour because I know what the Body did for me. Try it. See if it isn't better than an aspirin. Remember what Jesus did as you eat that bread and drink that juice or wine, whichever one you take.

I'm going to get mystical on you again. Take communion spiritually. As you eat the bread and drink the cup, see your spirit receiving it and spreading it to your soul and your body. See your soul receiving it where you are emotionally wounded. See your body receiving it where you need physical healing. Watch it stitch up the hurt and heal the wound.

You know by now what I'm going to say next. This can't be done on its own. You have to have the Word and the Spirit fully in you first.

Let's close this chapter with confessions:

Heavenly Father,

Forgive me for taking the Body and the Blood of my Lord Jesus Christ in a light-hearted, off-handed, insignificant or ritualistic manner.

I commit myself to making much of the Blood and the Body.

I will honor the great sacrifice of Jesus which did the mighty work for all mankind.

Forgive me for my lack of faith.

Help me to trust only in You.

Help me to lean on You at all times.

I will study the Blood, I will study the Body and I will honor them.

I will build my faith. I will no longer take my faith for granted.

Thank You for helping me do these things.

Amen.

Chapter 5

What About Death:
When Do We Stop Believing
for Someone Else's Healing?

One day on my rounds in the City of Faith I visited an elderly gentleman on his first day in the hospital; when I entered his room he appeared to be sleeping. His granddaughter invited me in. She stood on the opposite side of the bed, a woman in her mid-thirties.

"I'm the one who needs prayer!" she said fervently. "He's never been in the hospital before but he collapsed today. He lives in a retirement home and they couldn't revive him so they had an ambulance bring him here. I don't know what to do! He hasn't been conscious since this morning and the doctors say they're not sure what course of action to take.

"Actually, the doctors are being kind of secretive in my opinion but one nurse told me I might want to inform the family in case they want to say goodbye. What do I do? Granddad's 87. He's always been so healthy. What if it's a false alarm and I call the family and they spend all that money to fly out here...? Please ask the Lord what I should do!"

I picked up one of the gentleman's inert hands and asked the Lord for wisdom; then I waited. I heard these words in my spirit so I said them out loud. "Well done, good and faithful servant." The air in the room seemed to deflate. The woman said, "Thank you!" and hurried out to make her phone calls. Then the hand squeezed mine and went limp. I asked if there was anything else I should pray and the Spirit said "No." so I went on to my next patient.

Later in the day I saw the woman sitting in the lounge, her body as limp as that hand had been in mine. I came up behind her and touched her shoulder. "How's everything going?" I asked.

"Oh," she sighed. "Granddad died right after we left the room. The family is so grateful for that word from the Lord. He was a good and faithful servant. He served the Lord every day of his life for as long as anyone can remember."

That was the easiest death I went through. Some of you might be saying, "Yeah. And it was also the easiest call. 87. Living in a retirement home. It was time." And I say we can never be the judges of that. God looks at death differently than we do. He isn't waiting around for old age or for the grim reaper to cut us down. He's waiting for us to be satisfied and then He'll take us home.

Back in my hometown, before Bible school, I visited people in an old age home. One dear lady had been bedridden there for 15 years. Now ninety, she really wanted to die. She'd been a Christian since early childhood, so I, too, was curious as to why she was still on the earth.

I got her to talk about her life and in the process discovered that she was deathly afraid she was not forgiven. I explained about forgiveness being given at the moment of our new birth and that forgiveness applied to the past, the present and the future. But if we commit sins while being a Christian the Bible says the Lord is quick to forgive when we confess them.

She said a little prayer, admitting certain sins, and asked for forgiveness. When I left she seemed more settled or at peace, I couldn't quite put it into words. Two days later she died. She was satisfied.

"Precious in the sight of the Lord is the death of His saints" (Psalm 116:15).

There can be, of course, two meanings to this verse. Precious in the sight of the Lord is when His saints die to self and therefore belong to Him completely in this life. Or, precious in the sight of the Lord is when His saints physically die and join Him in heaven. In either case this Scripture rings true:

> *"So when this corruptible has put on incorruption, and this mortal has put on immortality, then shall be brought to pass the saying that is written: "Death is swallowed up in victory. O Death, where is your sting? O Hades, where is your victory? (1 Corinthians 15:54-55).*

The death that Satan has planned for us is gruesome, painful and debilitating. The death that God provides for us means simply to exit the body and enter the presence of God.

> *"For we know that if our earthly house, this tent, is destroyed, we have a building from God, a house not made with hands, eternal in the heavens. For in this we groan, earnestly desiring to be clothed with our habitation which is from heaven. So we are always confident, knowing that while we are at home in the body we are absent from the Lord. We are confident, yes, well pleased rather to be absent from the body and to be present with the Lord" (2 Corinthians 5:1-8).*

We have a choice in when we die. Notice how Paul says he is choosing.

"For to me, to live is Christ, and to die is gain. But if I live on in the flesh, this will mean fruit from my labor; yet what I shall choose I cannot tell. For I am hard-pressed between the two, having a desire to depart and be with Christ, which is far better. Nevertheless to remain in the flesh is more needful for you. And being confident of this, I know that I shall remain and continue with you all for your progress and joy of faith" (Philippians 1:21-25).

I have heard of saints who have announced to their families they would die that very day. They've gone to their favorite chair, appeared to have nodded off but in fact have left their bodies and joined the Lord. That's how I'm going to exit my body as well. No sickness and disease for me!

Maybe the gentleman in that hospital bed in the City of Faith had decided to die that day. Maybe not. Maybe he was waiting for someone to speak those parting words to him. Maybe not. But I do know he died right after he squeezed my hand. I saw his last breath leave his body.

On another occasion I went into a patient's room because he said yes when I asked if he wanted prayer, but his request shocked me. He asked me to pray he would die. In alarm I looked at his chart; he was exactly my age. I asked a few questions and he gave me his story.

For twenty years he had been in full-time ministry pastoring a sizeable Church. He had also been holding down a full-time job. His wife worked her own full-time job and their only child, a daughter, made them proud with her good grades and accomplishments.

He said, "I'm too tired. I want to go home. If I were twenty years younger I'd fight the good fight of faith, but I don't have the strength. I just want out of here and into heaven." I gathered from his other remarks that he worked so hard to keep his wife and daughter in a certain lifestyle while striving to obey God by being in the ministry. The insurance from his full time job would cover the continuation of that lifestyle. He had pioneered the church he pastored, had built it up to 500 people and had prepared someone for the Pastorate. In the natural his life was organized for death.

We, Prayer Partners, were trained not to impose our own opinions on the patients at all so I didn't know how to respond. Everything in me wanted to pray for his healing. He had only lived half his life, by my way of thinking, and circumstances could always change. But he was adamant. He wanted to die.

I asked if I could pray for rest and strength and come back tomorrow with an answer from the Lord, to which he agreed. That night I wrestled in prayer. Surely, God could change this man's heart! Finally at 4 a.m., that's when I seem to get most of my answers, the Lord spoke.

"Pray for the desires of his heart, not yours."

When I returned I quizzed him. What exactly were the desires of his heart? Pure and simple, he wanted death.

After my rounds I logged onto the computer in order to record my results. Normally, I didn't bother looking at other comments. When I first became a Prayer Partner I did until I realized we were all saying the same thing about each patient and then it got boring. However, this time I looked at what everyone else had prayed. All of them reported his desire for death and all of them reported they just couldn't bring themselves to pray for that so they prayed for peace, or other such soft responses.

I wrote, "I prayed for his death." I was afraid I might be kicked off the Prayer Partner team, but the only comments I received were congratulatory for my bravery. The morning of his scheduled surgery for the cancer, he was inexplicably found dead in his bed. His face was at peace.

Since then I have run into so many cases where the person wanted to die, but the loved ones around them prayed so hard that they kept them alive. Now the loved ones think they're doing a great thing, but the truth is the time they've gained, whether it is months or years, have proven to be the worst time of the patient's life.

One woman arranged with the Lord that she would die a certain day. She invited her family to come say goodbye (she was 91, by the way, and in Hospice care) and then went to sleep fully expecting to wake up in heaven. However, two women from her church went on a prayer vigil and stayed up all night demanding that she be kept on the earth. They did this because they thought they were pleasing her children. The woman woke up racked with pain from her crippling disease, which her faith had kept at bay up until that moment. She lived three horrific months before she died in excruciating pain.

A certain gentleman's wife lingered close to death strictly from weakness of old age. She was happy to die and go be with Jesus. He begged and pleaded with the Lord to keep her around as he needed her. She revived but shortly thereafter he died and shortly after that she succumbed to full blown Alzheimers! Nobody gained anything by her husband's prayers keeping her alive.

"He uncovers deep things out of darkness, and brings the shadow of death to light" (Job 12:22).

Let's face it, the deep things are between God and His child and the rest of us are not privy to that information unless one or the other reveals it to us. If God and His child have resolved that the child (speaking of adults) will die, let him or her go. Don't insert your will against the will of the person you're praying for, and especially not against the will of our Father!

I did experience the death of a child, although not my own. I'd always thought the death of a child to be the worst possible thing that could happen on earth. I discovered I was wrong.

An aunt of a little girl in Paris, beside herself in fear, begged me to visit her niece in the hospital. On my next trip to Paris I went. As I approached the room the Presence of the Lord felt almost tangible. Only one person at a time could be in the room and I had to be gowned in order to enter. My French wasn't good enough to comprehend the disease.

When I sat beside the little girl, she brightly told me all about heaven and pointed to the angels that were in her room. She said Jesus had come to take her home but she wanted to wait and say goodbye to her grandmother first. Jesus, apparently, waited patiently in the corner. I saw none of this but the spiritual atmosphere practically lifted me off my feet!

The mother waited for me outside. She asked, "She's going to die, isn't she?"

I responded, "She certainly wants to die."

Nodding she said, "I know." Her face clouded over but she whispered, "I'll let her go." And she did. The child died right after the grandmother's visit.

"As for me, I will see Your face in righteousness; I shall be satisfied when I awake in Your likeness" (Psalm 17:15).

I interpret this as meaning that when I am satisfied with life, then I will awake in God's likeness. When I have completed my race, accomplished all the Lord has laid out for me to do, when I've earned the prize of the high calling of Christ, then I will be ready to go home. Who on earth can say when that moment is for anybody except one's own self? Even for a child.

Not all death is so pretty. One day everybody on staff at City of Faith seemed to be in a dither when I arrived. A famous Pastor with an enormous church had been flown in from out of state. Neither the hospital in his state, nor City of Faith could stop the symptoms in his body from rapidly declining toward death.

The halls were filled with big name preachers who, having heard of the situation, flew into town, mostly in their private jets. They were walking up and down praying in loud voices, taking turns going into the room to lay hands on the Pastor. Wouldn't you know his name was on my list for the day!

I was terrified! I know now that it's not how you pray that counts, but how well you know the One to whom you are praying. However, I wondered at the time what little pipsqueak me could possibly pray in front of all these heavy hitting prayer warriors.

I went to the ladies room and had a little conversation with the Lord. I asked Him to give me the prayer that would get right to the heart of the problem and get it resolved because nothing seemed to be happening with all these big names in the hallway and the Pastor apparently was hours away from death.

The Lord told me He would tell me this one time what the problem was but I was never to ask again because the deep things belong to Him and His child. However, He would use this occasion to train me. He said the Pastor had unforgiveness in his heart which he refused to give up and therefore the Lord could do nothing for him.

I went to the door of the hospital room, told the Pastor I was a Prayer Partner and I asked him if I could come in and pray. He nodded yes. There were several big names in the room, but I ignored them and prayed the most effective prayer for healing I have ever uttered. Remember, prayer does not mean 'to ask for,' even though we are free to ask for anything, prayer means speaking and listening in conversation with God, so I was following instructions.

Then I asked the Pastor if I could pray for any unforgiveness in his heart. He started thrashing in his bed, scowled and growled, "I don't have any problems with that." I boldly said, "Well, just in case, let me pray for God to clean out your heart." He turned away, but I prayed anyway. I mean, hours away from death! I'm going to do the max of what God says! Within a few hours he did die and his face was not peaceful.

We determine our own deaths, even if we succumb to Satan. If he gets to choose how we die, it's because we've allowed him to have that authority. We can die early; we can die in an accident. The Bible seems to suggest that these unfortunate deaths can be traced back to sin or foolishness, both of which are sponsored by Satan and both of which we choose.

Death is the threshold to heaven. It is not defeat; not for a Christian. Satan wants to kill us before we're finished here, that's why there are so many Scriptures against death. But a timely death when the person is satisfied and steps over easily is a glorious event.

Keep these Scriptures in your heart:

"I shall not die, but live, and declare the works of the Lord" *(Psalm 118:17).*

"...I have come that they may have life and that they may have it more abundantly" *(John 10:10).*

"Do not be overly wicked, nor be foolish; why should you die before your time?" (Ecclesiastes 7:17).

"Jesus said to her, "I am the resurrection and the life. He who believes in Me, though he may die, he shall live. And whoever lives and believes in Me shall never die. Do you believe this?" (John 11:25-26).

Chapter 6

The Healings of Jesus

The first healing that John reports is of the nobleman's son. In it he states the case of the Church today, the mentality of anointing versus faith, and in case you miss his point, which I know you won't, I will capitalize it for you anyway!

> *"So Jesus came again to Cana of Galilee where He had made the water wine. And there was a certain nobleman whose son was sick at Capernaum. When he heard that Jesus had come out of Judea into Galilee, he went to Him and implored Him to come down and heal his son, for he was at the point of death. Then Jesus said to him, "UNLESS YOU PEOPLE SEE SIGNS AND WONDERS, YOU WILL BY NO MEANS BELIEVE. The nobleman said to Him, "Sir, come down before my child dies! Jesus said to him, "Go your way, your son*

lives." So the man believed the word that Jesus spoke to him and he went his way. And as he was now going down, his servants met him and told him, saying, "Your son lives!" (John 4:46-51).

The story of the leper demonstrates Jesus' attitude about healing.

"And behold, a leper came and worshipped Him, saying, "Lord, if You are willing, You can make me clean." Then Jesus put out His hand and touched him, saying, "I AM WILLING; be cleansed." Immediately his leprosy was cleansed" (Matthew 8:2-3).

Continuing through the Gospels, the Centurion came to Jesus for healing for his servant. First Jesus marvels at the man's faith saying he has never seen such <u>great faith</u> in all of Israel.

"Then Jesus said to the centurion, "Go your way, and as you have <u>believed</u>, so let it be done for you" (Matthew 8:13).

A paralytic was brought to Jesus lying on a bed carried by his friends.

"When Jesus saw their <u>faith</u>, He said to the paralytic, "Son, be of good cheer; your sins are forgiven you. 7 And he arose and departed to his house" (Matthew 9:2, 7).

A woman who had a flow of blood for twelve years stepped out of a crowd and touched the hem of Jesus' garment.

>*"But Jesus turned around, and when He saw her He said, "Be of good cheer, daughter, your <u>faith</u> has made you well" (Matthew 9:22).*

On His way to lay hands on Jairus' daughter, who was at the point of death, servants from Jairus' house came running up saying not to bother the Master any longer as the girl was dead.

>*"As soon as Jesus heard the word that was spoken, He said to the ruler of the synagogue (Jairus), "Do not be afraid. Only <u>believe</u>. 42 Immediately the girl arose and walked, for she was twelve years of age. And they were overcome with great amazement" (Mark 5:36, 42).*

Two blind men approached Jesus asking Him to have mercy on them.

>*"And when He had come into the house the blind men came to Him. And Jesus said to them, "Do you <u>believe</u> that I am able to do this?" They said to him, "Yes, Lord." Then He touched their eyes, saying, "According to your <u>faith</u> let it be to you. And their eyes were opened" (Matthew 9:28-30).*

A father brought his epileptic son to Jesus and explained his son's fits asking Him to help them.

> *"Jesus said to him, "If you can <u>believe</u>, all things are possible to him who <u>believes</u>. Jesus took him by the hand and lifted him up, and he arose" (Mark 9:23, 27).*

When blind Bartimaeus came to Jesus, people tried to shut him up, but he continued to cry out. Jesus asked what he wanted and Bartimaeus said he wanted to receive his sight.

> *"Then Jesus said to him, "Go your way, your <u>faith</u> has made you well." And immediately he received his sight and followed Jesus on the road" (Mark 10:52).*

The story of the ten lepers, according to my conjecture, shows the difference between how the Lord treats the world and how He treats His own. Ten lepers called to Jesus from afar as they were not allowed to approach people. They called out for mercy. He answered that they were to go and show themselves to the priests, according to Jewish law. Apparently the leprosy left them.

One, however, a Samaritan, returned to worship Jesus and to thank Him.

> *"So Jesus answered and said, "Were there not ten cleansed? But where are the nine? Were there not any found who returned to give glory to God except this foreigner? And He said to him, "Arise, go*

your way. Your <u>faith</u> has made you whole" (Luke 17:17-19).

God provides healing for everyone. If you leave something alone long enough it will heal itself, rarely like it was before, but usable. A broken bone, for example, if not properly set, will eventually become whole again, but the filaments of bone cells will have created a knob where the bone has mended, however, the bone will be usable.

Conversely, leprosy eats away the flesh. When the nine were healed the leprosy went away but the destruction of the disease left gouges and malformation. Some probably went to the priests without noses or some went without fingers or toes. But the one who gave himself to Jesus, because one cannot worship without first surrendering oneself to the object of worship, he was made whole. I believe his nose and fingers and toes grew back, the malformation corrected itself and the gouges filled in.

I have just given you eight healings straight from the Bible that were based on faith. Even in those healings that do not mention faith, or believing, never does Scripture record Jesus saying something like: "Boy, are you guys lucky that I came along with this powerful anointing." Not once does He refer to His power. It's true that out of His compassion He now and then healed people, like the woman bent over for 18 years, the man in the Pharisee's house who had Dropsy or the blind man in whose eyes he put His spit. However, Jesus' consistent response was to attribute healing to a person's faith.

Chapter 7

Will He find Faith?

I hope the message of this book comes through to you loud and clear because the Lord is giving me an urgency in my spirit to explain it as well as I possibly can. You are His beloved. He wants you to have every gift He purchased for you at such a high price. No husband buys his wife an expensive gift and then enjoys seeing her stash it in the closet and never use it. Jesus is your Husband. He adores you. Give Him pleasure and use His gift!

Healing belongs to Christians. Learn to receive it by faith. Rise up and take it. Don't let any demon from hell, or any well-intentioned human being, talk you out of it. Jesus paid a heavy price to give you healing so honor the gift, reverence it and apply it to your life. Have high intention where healing is concerned. Determine that you will not stop until you have received it. Be vehement in taking it by force!

> *"But although He had done so many signs before them, they did not believe in Him, that the word of Isaiah the prophet might be fulfilled, which he spoke: "Lord, who has believed our report? And to whom has the arm of the Lord been revealed?"* (John 12:37-38).

Whose report will you believe? This is a critical matter. Jesus wants to know.   Will you believe the report of the skeptics around you? Will you believe the report of Satan? Or will you have faith in Jesus, not only that He exists, but that He paid the price for your SALVATION? That His Blood paid for your sins? That His Body paid for your sicknesses, diseases, distresses and pains? Will you put your whole trust in Him? I pray to God we can all say YES!

> *"... Nevertheless, when the Son of Man comes, will He really find faith on the earth?"* (Luke 18:8).

A Message from the Author

You are perfect you. No one can be more perfectly you than you are. God made you completely unique so there can be no duplicate, no substitute. He made you for Himself and He knows you because there is nobody else like you.

Yes, you have two natures. When the sperm from your father joined the egg from your mother, one nature came into being which governs your body and your soul. This nature is a fallen one, inherited from all your generations back to the original sin.

When that sperm and egg became one, more was created than a stem cell. At conception God breathed into you your spirit which is your divine nature, a portion of the Spirit of God. God is Love and God is Light. Your spirit is made of love and light.

About the age of twelve a certain portion of your brain began its appointed time of development: the ability to reason and make decisions on your own. You, like everyone else, learned you could choose between good and evil – not just be naughty or nice – but to choose evil and you found you could, at least for awhile, live with its consequences. Or you could choose good and receive its gracious and glorious rewards.

Unfortunately, choosing evil overrode your conscience, the gateway to your spirit. You seared your conscience and the door between the fallen nature and the divine nature stood open like a rusty gate. Sadly, your divine nature became corrupt like your fallen nature.

You can't just clean up a corrupt spirit; you have to exchange it for a new one. How is that possible? God already gave you your portion of His Spirit. So how do you get another one? You accept the gift of Jesus Christ. He came to take your place, to pay for what you did wrong, to erase your sins and give you a portion of His Spirit.

He blew on His disciples, they received His Spirit and became born again. He continues to breathe on new believers today. Whenever anyone says, "Jesus, I have sinned against You, Your Father and the Kingdom of God..." (see the rest of this prayer at the end of this discourse) and sincerely means it, Jesus will give him or her a new spirit.

You can be born again. Once you have received your new birth you can get your soul saved and your body will follow suit because your body does whatever your soul tells it to do. How do you get your soul saved? Obeying the Spirit of God with a willing heart one step at a time cleans up your soul and works your salvation from the inside, where your spirit man is, through the soul, your mind, emotions and will, to the outside to be expressed in your body.

Only those who receive Jesus as Lord today will live tomorrow in the Kingdom of God forever. Those who do not receive Him as their Lord will spend eternity in the kingdom of darkness. Choose today. Start your Eternal Life by giving yourself to Jesus and making Him your Lord. Love and Light will once again reside in your new spirit and He will give you His abundant life.

THE SINNER'S PRAYER

Jesus, I have sinned against You, Your Father and the Kingdom of God. I've made a mess of things by trying to run my own life and running away from you. Please forgive me. Please apply the blood You so painfully shed to pay for my sins to my spirit, soul and body. I receive You now, Jesus, as my Savior, my Lord, my best Friend, my Master and my Commander in Chief. I will love You, I will serve You, I will honor You, I will proclaim You all the days of my life and I will live with You for eternity in Heaven, the Kingdom of Love.

Thank You, Jesus! I am Yours! Amen.

MORE BOOKS
by Marty Delmon

DESTINED FOR SUCCESS
www.rpjandco.com

Isaiah foretold the cross, the price Jesus would pay and the benefits we would receive. He mentioned prosperity. "The chastisement of our prosperity was upon Him," Is 53:5. The Hebrew word is SHALOM! While the translators used the word 'peace' in this verse, both prosperity and peace are the meanings of SHALOM. The two words are interchangeable. Can you have peace without prosperity? Doesn't prosperity bring peace? Jesus paid for you to have prosperity. It's a new-birth right. DESTINED FOR SUCCESS defines that prosperity and directs you to the path to receive it. SHALOM!

DESTINED FOR LOVE
www.rpjandco.com

In DESTINED FOR LOVE, Author Marty Delmon takes you on a journey through the Bible to demonstrate what love is, how to use it and what amazing results are intrinsically woven into the practice of love. Love is a force. Without a doubt it is the strongest force on the earth.

Probe the depth, the breadth, the length and the height of this heavenly love. In the pages of DESTINED FOR LOVE Delmon teaches how to receive this all-consuming love, how to stay filled and how to give it away without ever becoming deplenished. It's yours. Heaven never tires of loving you.

Christians are DESTINED FOR LOVE. The question is will you fulfill your destiny? Will you find the source of all good things coming down from the Father of Lights? The promises of God are all based on love. In honesty you have to answer the question: are you having trouble receiving what you need and want from God? Love first comes from heaven to your heart. Then you use that love to love others. Plainly said, your problem with love may be wrapped up in your inability to receive God's profound love for you -- first. Be loved, beloved. You are DESTINED FOR LOVE!

DESTINED FOR FAITH
www.rpjandco.com

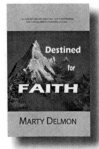

What is it that makes a Christian's life different from that of a person who doesn't believe in Jesus Christ the Son of God? Gosh, where to begin? There can be a long list, but it really boils down to one thing. We trust God.

The major benefit of having faith is huge! Something dynamic comes from God our Father and that power delivers to us what we believe for God to provide. It is by faith that we draw what we want into our natural, physical life. God doesn't just want us to have "pie in the sky in the sweet by and by!" He wants us to have "steak on our plate while we wait!" Only faith can bring that pie out of the sky and make it become steak on our plate. This takes a profound level of trust that is not for the lukewarm. It's an all or nothing faith. Sure we can do it. It's just a matter of answering this question: do we want it bad enough?"

This book will instruct the reader in how to turn life into an adventure of faith, the kind of faith that moves God. The Bible says it's faith that pleases Him. The Lord wants to change our world through our faith. That's what makes Him happy.

DESTINED FOR GRACE
www.rpjandco.com

Grace is Favor, Favor is Grace. Don't you love to have Favor wherever you go? Doors open for you; things happen to your benefit; prosperity flows; healing breaks forth; all things work together for your good. Well, you do have Favor. Jesus brought God's Grace to you as a new-birth-day gift. You just have to learn to walk in it. You've been carefully taught how to walk in worldly ways and to gain the favor of man, but that only goes so far and usually costs a lot. The Favor of God cost Jesus a lot but to you the Grace of God has been freely given. How to walk in the ways of Grace is the subject of this book as it teaches you how to use the divine Favor you have already been given. Whatever you need, or even want, if you can find it in the Word of God then you know He has already made a way for you to have it. Divine Grace gives you above and beyond anything you can ask or think! Believe it! Receive it! Walk in it!

Books from Tate Publishing
www.tatepublishing.com

Buried Lies

Sleeping with
Demons

Buried Lies
Companion Workbook

Wild Card

Buried Lies Companion
Audio Book

Wildfire

"WRITE!" He rumbled -- the voice He uses when I dawdle. Standing with hundreds, responding to the altar call for "Ministers who feel like square pegs in a round hole," I suddenly knew what to do: Lead people to Christ by writing short stories and putting them on the radio. Quitting the Pastorate, I began. A small radio station taught me everything and now, writing, recording and producing evangelistic stories is the thrust of my ministry.

In seven French speaking countries over 100 stations transmit more than 300 stories (so far). I send them one 15 minute program a week, but they broadcast them multiple times a week at prime time! Why? Because the lost are calling wanting to know how they can find this Jesus to help them with their lives like He helped whatever character they just heard.

It costs $300 to produce one story. That takes it from translation, recording, music, sound effects, duplication, to mailing them to the stations. If 364 churches, or individuals, or corporations pay for one story a year, we can reach the world in seven languages. Whoever sponsors a story with $300, their name, city and state is written into the credits and whenever that master CD is copied, wherever it is broadcast, the listeners will know who cared enough for the lost to send the Gospel.

I have more writing projects sitting on my heart than I probably have years to live. However, I'm hard at work at it. For instance, I'm writing a new novel entitled Raw Truth, I've written a couple of screenplays, one about Buried Lies. Anybody know an agent? Then I've got an evangelistic TV series on my heart....

Since I need sponsors to get these works around the world, I offer you the possibility of participating with me. **To receive a tax-deduction please send an offering to World Missions Ministries, P.O. Box 12609, OKC, OK 73157 and put 31051m on the memo line.** You'll receive a book from me, a tax deductible letter from WMM and my prayers for God's recompense for your obedience. The Lord bless you, keep you and give you His peace!

About the Publisher

In 2004, the Spirit of God birthed RPJ & Company according to Romans 14:17.

RPJ & Company, Inc. began publishing Christian books for pastors, leaders, ministers, missionaries, and others with a message to help the Body of Christ. Our published books continue to empower, inspire and motivate people to aspire to a higher level of understanding through the written word.

Our company is dedicated to assisting those individuals who desire to publish Christian books that are uplifting, inspiring and self-help in nature. We also offer assistance for those who would like to self-publish.

The special service that we provide is customized, quality layout and design for every client. This gives every new author a chance at becoming successfully-published. For every book, we offer exposure and a worldwide presence to help the book and the author become discovered!

"As an author and publisher, I can guide you through the steps of creating, editing, proofreading and providing you with a professional layout and design for any printed item, one you'll be proud to call your own."

- Kathleen Schubitz
Founder and CEO

RPJ & COMPANY, INC.
"Where quality and excellence meet face to face!"

www.rpjandco.com / www.store.rpjandco.com

CPSIA information can be obtained at www.ICGtesting.com
Printed in the USA
LVOW090641200212

269456LV00001B/14/P